THE MAGIC AND POWER OF EMOTIONAL INTELLIGENCE

Try to find the Courage to be Wise,
to make Wise, compassionate choices,

Try to be free from hostility, affliction
and anxiety.

Live happily!.

"A drop of Wisdom,
better than an ocean of gold".

January 2024, Oxford.

AESOP Wisdom books:

*Aesop's Fables: A New Edition of the Townsend Version
with Preface and Introduction by Susie Moore*

(2018)

The Lost Wisdom Property Office

(2018)

THE MAGIC AND POWER OF EMOTIONAL INTELLIGENCE

For Our Young People

Yania Braun

AESOP Wisdom
Oxford

AESOP Wisdom

First edition published by AESOP Wisdom

5 Broadlands House, Mill Lane, Oxford OX3 0FQ
ninajanina03@gmail.com

A catalogue record of this book is
available from the British Library.

ISBN: 979-8-777063-92-2

CONTENTS

The wisdom of the wise and the experience
of the ages are perpetuated by quotations
Benjamin Disraeli

I pick my favourite quotations and store them in my mind
as ready armour, offensive or defensive, amid the struggle
of this turbulent existence
Robert Burns

The quotations when engraved upon the memory
give you good thoughts. They also make you anxious to
read the authors and look for more.
Winston Churchill

*Youth is about beauty
and growing up pains.*

*This book is dedicated
to all young people everywhere.*

*Growing up is about being hurt.
People can be unkind.*

Never lose hope that things will get better.

*If your heart didn't know pain,
it wouldn't know any great love either*

With love,
  from Yasmia. x

Preface

Emotional intelligence – emotional intuition – wisdom about 'how to live' is forever changing our concept of 'being smart'. Animals are smart, people are wise. 'Emotionally intelligent' means having the wisdom, intuition and empathy to sense how another person might feel in any given situation. For example, emotionally intelligent people will not tell lies because they know how it can affect the person to whom they tell the lie. An emotionally intelligent person is a good, wise person.

> 'I don't care how much you know,
> Until I know how much you care.'

Emotional intelligence can determine life success more than IQ. An emotionally intelligent leader will inspire, stimulate passion and enthusiasm, will keep people motivated and committed, and their company will thrive. Toxic leadership can 'poison' the emotional climate of a workplace.

In moments of human tragedy and crisis, emotional intelligence will be about empathy, love, compassion and understanding. It will also help in finding meaning and sense in the face of chaos and madness, by putting into words what everyone is feeling in their hearts.

Emotionally intelligent, self-aware leaders will speak openly about their emotions, will know their strengths and limitations, will welcome constructive criticism and feedback, and will know when to ask for help.

Emotional intelligence will also benefit our family life, our marriages, our children, our communities. *Emotionally intelligent* people with self-control will stay calm and clear-headed during crisis.

Emotional intelligence is *Wisdom!*

Yania Braun, 2021

The best hope of a nation
lies in the proper education of its youth.
Erasmus

We need knowledge that will profit society,
will improve moral and economic status,
the knowledge that is both useful and social,
knowledge about honour, dignity, happiness etc.
School plays a big part in it, we need
enthusiastic teachers
Benjamin Franklin,*
The Worst American

---

* Benjamin Franklin gave up his profitable business at the age of 41, and was happiest to meet and talk to people about life and wisdom of living. He published the *Little Richard* magazine about the wisdom of living and said, 'Be aware of little expenses', 'Fish and visitors smell after a few days', and other practical pieces of wisdom.

THE ELEVEN PILLARS OF EMOTIONAL INTELLIGENCE

1. Emotional intelligence – emotional intuition – wisdom about 'how to live' – is forever changing our concept of 'being smart'.

2. Emotionally intelligent people will have wisdom, intuition about people's emotions in any given situation.

3. Emotionally intelligent people won't tell a hungry person, 'I'm going to have my dinner now.' They will know how it would make a hungry man feel. This is also called 'tact' and 'tactful behaviour'.

4. An emotionally intelligent person is a good, wise person:
     'I don't care how much you know,
     Until I know how much you care.'

5. Emotionally intelligent leaders will inspire, stimulate passion and enthusiasm, and will keep people motivated and committed.

6. Why? Because they will understand how people feel and what matters to them.

7. Toxic leadership can poison the emotional climate of a workplace.

8. Some leaders love power and control – and don't care about employees.

9. In moments of human tragedy, crisis, emotional intelligence will be about empathy, love, compassion, understanding.

10. Emotionally intelligent bosses will talk to their employees to help them understand and find meaning in a crisis to appreciate how everybody feels, while staying calm and clear-headed.

11. Emotionally intelligent bosses are wise bosses: they have wisdom in their heart and knowledge in their head.

Introduction

The greatness lies in being kind
True Wisdom is a happy mind

THIS BOOK is about sharing the experience of being human in our modern world.

The messages in it come from different people – 'small', ordinary, famous, rich, etc. You're asked to think and reason in your own mind, and find your own truth, Wisdom and happiness.

I guess it's the only modern book of its kind. It was not written in any particular order, and you do not need to read it from beginning to end. It was written without any plan at all, but instead has been compiled with lots of love for young people. I do hope the book will become your companion for life, the best friend you could ever have. Think about it!

I am very curious about human lives, about

emotions and the motives behind what people do. It would be safe to say that we're all a bit mad, and some of us realise it. No one is perfect: we are only human and come from different backgrounds.

The expression 'being smart' is being replaced by 'having emotional intelligence'. An emotionally intelligent person is a good, wise person who will understand people's emotions in any given situation.

'I don't care how much you know
until I know how much you care.'

I do hope you will enjoy the book, and please remember to share it with your friends.

Thank you,

Yania x

AESOP

VERY LITTLE is known about the legendary, ancient Greek writer whose stories of clever animals are first and foremost morality tales. Aesop was born a slave; he lived in Samoa in the sixth century BC and was given his freedom by his second master for his Wisdom and wit. The word 'Wisdom' is about 2,500 years old. When *Aesop's Fables* was properly published in 1475–80, no book, with the exception of the Holy Scriptures, had a wider circulation. Let's talk about Wisdom and let's use the word Wisdom.

WISDOM, GOODNESS AND BEAUTY

Wisdom is goodness and beauty. Wise people live good, honest lives. Wisdom will give use meaningful lives by showing us what really matters.

WISDOM AND HEALTH

Wise people are cheerful and live longer. Wisdom has the power to heal our troubled world. A wise, confident, happy man will never dream of hurting others. Wisdom will give us Health:

- physical – no stress-related pain
- emotional – understanding our emotions
- mental – sharing our worries and fears with people we trust, to avoid depression, suicide

WISDOM IS FREE

Wisdom is free, just love it, learn it and live it. Our young people need our guidance with love and logic – golden legacy from parents, grandparents, teachers, etc.

LIFE AND LIVING

Life is easy and simple, but living can be difficult sometimes, when we ask ourselves: what shall I do? We can't always control what happens to us, but we can choose how to react to it.

WISDOM AND MIND

Wisdom is about thinking, reasoning, about our Mind. The way we think; the way we feel. Our Mind can be our biggest enemy. Have you ever seen a sad flower or depressed tree? They don't have a mind that that would make them sad or depressed. Would you agree?

FORGIVE YOURSELF

'I've messed up', people often say. Forgive yourself – you didn't do it intentionally. If there's a chance, say sorry and mean it. It might not be too late! Learning Wisdom about life and living is the answer to almost everything. Wisdom is goodness and beauty!

ENJOY GROWING OLD

A wise person will enjoy growing old: 'because it took me a while to get rid of the ideas that I had about myself, that weren't helpful. I feel much happier now.'

WISDOM AND EASE

Wisdom will teach us that it is always possible to allow some ease into even the most challenging situations. Our young people need to train their minds to be positive and realistic.

PASSION, ENTHUSIASM AND LOVE

We need passion, enthusiasm and love for learning about Wisdom. It will give us strength in all life's situations. Wisdom comes before money, wealth, fame, degrees, social status, good looks, etc.

WISDOM AND KNOWLEDGE

Knowledge is not Wisdom. We need Wisdom to know how to use well our knowledge, our fame, our power, our money – even our good looks!

STAR TREATMENT

]
A famous singer said: 'I'm getting star treatment because I'm earning big money but I was the same man when I was poor.' Does fame tell us that people are gullible? It's not about his singing, it's about the money he earns.

GOOD LOOKS

Good looks are God given – no achievement in them – why should you be famous for being pretty or good looking. How shallow, you could say!

WISDOM AND ANSWERS

Wisdom won't have answers to everything. We can't understand the Universe and have to accept that life gives us no certainty. Wisdom will warn us about unnecessary risks to protect us from being disappointed.

EINSTEIN'S WISDOM

Here is Albert Einstein's Wisdom while answering the question 'Why are we here?'

'Strange is our situation here upon earth. Each of us comes for a short visit, not knowing why, yet sometimes seeming to a divine purpose. From the standpoint of daily life, however, there is one thing we do know: That we are here for the sake of other men – above all for those upon whose smile and well-being our own happiness depends, for the countless unknown souls with whose fate we are connected by a bond of sympathy. Many times a day, I realize how much my outer and inner life is built upon the labours of people, both living and dead, and how earnestly I must exert myself in order to give in return as much as I have received and am still receiving.'

OUR FREE WILL

To turn to evil ways and be wicked
To turn to good ways and be good
We can choose the path to follow
To be learned or ignorant
To be mean or generous
To be merciful or cruel
We need humility and tenderness of the heart.

CONSCIENCE

Man is the only creature that possesses Conscience, the voice which calls him back to himself, back to himself. It helps him to remain aware of the goals of his life and the ways that are necessary to fulfil those goals. A clear conscience is a soft pillow.

PROBLEMS

Only fools have no problems or worries and they live in a 'fool's paradise'. Problems make life interesting. Moreover they make us think and reason and learn Wisdom. Overcoming our problems adds meaning to our lives. Don't worry too much. Don't avoid problems – you will be OK!

RACISM

How can we solve racism? We need to educate our new generation to understand it and try to make a difference.

- ✦ We are all children of God.
- ✦ To be different makes us special.
- ✦ We don't know why we are black or white.
- ✦ Should we blame God?
- ✦ What we don't change we have to accept; anything else would be madness.
- ✦ No matter what colour, we all have two things in common:

➤ we all want to be happy and not suffer;
➤ we were all born the same way and will die the same way!

TEACHING WISDOM

It should start at home, on mother's knee, as they say, where our kind, loving, caring parents will tell us:

✦ You're as good as others, if not better.
✦ You can do anything in life, if you try hard enough.
✦ Take no notice of unkind people.
✦ We believe in you, and are here for you always.

SELF-WORTH AND SELF-ESTEEM

These are the keys to everything in life, to a happy life and success. Our children need to know:

✦ They are of value
✦ They are lovable
✦ They are able

USEFUL KNOWLEDGE

Benjamin Franklin said: 'We need Knowledge that will profit society, will improve moral and economic status. The Knowledge that is both useful and social. Knowledge about *honour*, *dignity*, *happiness*, etc. *School* plays a big part in it. We need *enthusiastic teachers*.'

DEALING WITH PEOPLE

The most difficult job in life is dealing with people, young or old. It's more difficult than coping with losing all you have in a fire or a flood. Material things and money can be replaced. People's attitudes and insecurities can cause us a lot of pain.

WHO ARE 'EVIL' PEOPLE?

They were born like the rest of us, beautiful and innocent. Society let them down, not paying attention to their emotional needs when they were growing up. They often grow into angry adults, craving revenge. They hate everything around them. Some have murderous thoughts.

THERE ARE THREE GROUPS OF PEOPLE

- some are born with wise genes,
- some are weak and follow others
- some are born with angry genes

TRUE ACHIEVEMENT

Success in life is a quality of our mind and character, and it's called Wisdom. Being rich, beautiful, famous, powerful is no big deal. You can lose all that, but nobody can take away from you what you put in your head and your heart. Even if you lose everything you had – you still have yourself, your mind and character.

PSYCHOPATHS

Have you ever met someone who was charming, convincing and poisonous? Keep away from them – they can be dangerous! Have a modest doubt about anyone you meet.

THE 'LOVE GAME'

Some people know how to play the 'love game', and it's so easy to be blinded by it. Refuse to send any money to someone who emails you saying 'I love you'. At the same time, refuse an invitation to a hotel from a person you don't know well. A beautiful, young British graduate was murdered by a charming young stranger in a hotel room in New Zealand. She knew him for a couple of days only! Modest doubt about everything is the beacon of the wise.

CERTAINTY

Certainty is what humans crave most, but sadly we have many questions and no answers. It's impossible to understand everything! We just have to trust our instinct and hope for the best.

CHEATS

Once a cheat, always a cheat – what do you think? I would like to think that people can change, but do they? They like themselves as they are, and simply don't care about the rest. They simply don't know any better. Can you blame them?

A WOMAN IN LOVE

A woman in love never takes advice. The beauty of first love – we think it will last forever. Can you blame a teenager who was told for the first time in their life, 'I love you!' A teenage child with an absent parent. To be 'in love' feels great – and not to mention sex! How do they know anything about love in the real world? Teenage pregnancies and single mums – it's all so sad!

ANGER

Acting out our anger. Slamming the door behind us! What happens if one day later you would like to come back? A wise man says: 'Never burn the bridges, leave the door open, so you can come back. It's your home, you belong there, and your family, even if not perfect, is your family forever!

PEOPLE PLEASER

People often abuse your kindness and it makes you unhappy and disappointed. 'How could they do that to me?' we often ask ourselves. The answer is: 'Simply, easily – that's what people do!' Don't be too kind to people who don't deserve it and remember to keep your boundaries.

LEARN TO SAY 'NO'

Do it a few times and it will become second nature to you. The good thing is, you don't have to invent any excuses – just simply say, 'Sorry, can't do it.' Full stop. Courage to say NO to people will give you a lot of confidence and a happier life.

IF YOUTH KNEW, IF AGE COULD...

They say that youth is wasted on the young. Maybe it's true: young people lack wisdom and don't even see the beauty of their youth. Old people understand life better and often wish they could be young again. It is a bit sad that we're only young once! Nothing can be done about it. The sweet ironies of life!

IF ONLY WE HAD KNOWN

At twenty, we worry about what others think of us. At forty, we don't care. At sixty, we discover that nobody was thinking about us at all. Why worry? If only we had known!

BEWARE

Have you ever met a person like this one: he agrees with everything you say, he's charming. He is either a fool or he's getting ready to scam you. Always have a modest doubt about people you meet for the first time.

WE JUST NEED TO NOTICE

Everything in life has its wonders – we just need to notice them. Do you realise how special it is to hold your child's hand, for example? Our thinking, feeling and acting can be so rich, so happy! It's all up to us. It's our choice.

PEACE IN YOUR HEART

Pain and sadness can have their wonder too. We can learn to forgive others and forgive ourselves and it can enrich our life. Have you ever experienced that? To forgive your enemy? When you forgive yourself, you will have peace in your heart. You can forget about something that wasn't making you happy. Peace of mind and peace in your heart – the greatest gifts you can give to yourself. We don't have to be strong and wise all the time.

WHAT A LITTLE OLD LADY TOLD ME

A little old lady told me the following story:

A plumber who came to do a small job for me looked like a 'nice man', and I trusted him. I was wrong. Why? He overcharged me, taking advantage of the fact that I was an old lady, living on her own. I felt sad and challenged him, without success. It was playing on my mind and I couldn't forget his face. One day later I decided to forgive him, and I did. It felt great! I remembered the wise saying: 'Bad people ought to be pitied, not hated. Greedy people have money, and that's all they have. Forgiveness is a beautiful thing with a 'who cares' attitude!

NOT EVERYTHING IN LIFE IS BAD

There's goodness and beauty; people are good at heart. The latest pandemic was all about caring and kindness – humanity at its best. This should give us hope and courage to face life cheerfully.

ONE DRINK TOO MANY

What would you say about the statement, 'What a man says drunk, he thought when sober'? It could be true. I smile at my childhood memories: when my father had one drink too many, he would complain about one of my mother's friends, who he said he 'hated'. Did he really? The next morning he wouldn't remember any of it! They say that alcohol gives you 'courage' to say how you feel.

THE POWER OF THE MIND

A wise man said that our mind and thoughts can make Heaven out of Hell and Hell out of Heaven. If we think happy, we feel happy and act happy. Let's remember Oscar Wilde's famous words here:

> 'We're all in the gutter,
> But some of us are looking at the stars.'

THE POWER OF THE WHISPER

I love this piece of wisdom and make use of it almost every time while talking to an angry person. If your child is angry, whisper to them. It usually has the desired effect of calming them down. With an angry stranger, I just speak quietly – it confuses them. I don't allow anybody's anger including my own to become destructive.

DON'T HOLD GRUDGES

If you resent your friend and their partner for one reason or another, don't hold the grudge for too long. Why? Because while you torture yourself, they might be out dancing. Who cares how you feel? Why should they care? So why should you care? A wise man says; 'Resentment is like taking a poison, and waiting for your enemy to die.' Be good to yourself – you can go dancing with your partner as well!

LOVE AND COMPASSION

It's our duty to raise the capacity for love and compassion in our children. They will grow into kind, compassionate adults and will make us proud. They will be wise and not interested in hurting others. This way our society, families and the world can be healed. Children learn fast and if they learn properly, they will always remember it like they do their A–Z alphabet.

ANGER AND BEING ALIVE

Anger can be a good emotion when we know what to do with it. Not being happy about something will motivate us to do something about it. Anger is also a sign that we are alive. Don't feel bad about being angry sometimes! And one more thing: should you ever 'waste' your anger on a fool, don't give him satisfaction!

TEACHING A PIG

Never try to teach a pig to dance or sing – it will waste your time, and you will upset a pig.

ENDING AN ARGUMENT

In my home we've got a system for ending an argument. We talk and talk, until my partner is right!

GRATITUDE

Never fall out with your bread and butter. Good days start with gratitude. It's so easy to forget the kindnesses we receive from other people, especially members of our family. Even 'bad' family is still a family for us. We mustn't take it for granted. Some of us in this world have nobody at all to call a family. It must be pretty sad and lonely.

DISPUTE

Have you ever had a long, not too important dispute with your neighbour? Would you be ready to 'surrender'? Probably both of you are wrong. Wouldn't you like your mind to be at peace? A wise old man said, 'A neighbour over the fence is more important than a brother abroad.'

INACTION

Inaction can be the highest form of action. Wisdom is patient. Sleep on it. If anyone upsets you, write them a 'kind' letter and put it in a bottom drawer. It will calm your nerves. You will sleep well, and tomorrow you may feel differently. With a quiet mind you will be able to think rationally and benefit from it.

NOBILITY IN LABOUR

Maybe you hate your job and it doesn't make much sense to you to get up every morning and do the same 'boring' things all day. Something is missing here. A young man said: 'My father taught me to work hard, but forgot to teach me to enjoy it!' How very true. We have to believe that there's nobility in every labour – ploughing a field or writing a poem. Do you also think that every politician, doctor, lawyer, nurse, teacher is excited going to work every day? Every one of us contributes in a special way, we must remember that. Not having a job can be very difficult too. Try to think about your attitude towards the job you do for a living.

ROUTINE

Has anyone ever told you that 'life is largely routine' and we can't feel happy, inspired, excited all the time. Sometimes it doesn't feel right and life can even seem boring and depressing. Imagine a young woman with her first baby – how tiring, how boring, can I have some sleep... Feeding a baby throughout the day and night, baby cries and you don't know why, giving it a bath, changing nappies. Post-natal depression is only too understandable! You are very lucky if you can be helped so you can have a nap during the day. But let's look on the bright side: babies grow fast, too fast: they learn to walk and talk, and one day will go to school and you will miss them and find you have too much time on your hands. Ordinary everyday routines lead to extraordinary results – we just need to persevere!

EINSTEIN AND WORK

Albert Einstein said: 'Work is the only thing that adds substance to life.' He did work very hard and long hours. Would you be happy to have his job? I'm sure Einstein had bad days too.

TEACHING BY EXAMPLE

You may have a boring, miserable job, but it pays your bills and rent, drinks at the pub, and food on the table. Things are never as bad as they appear. Our children will learn from us the value of work when they grow up. Teaching by example is best.

EINSTEIN AND FAME

The great Einstein loved his equations. He wasn't interested in being famous. He laughed at it: 'And with fame I become more and more stupid, but of course it's a very common phenomenon.' He was disappointed with life and people. At 75 he refused any medical treatment that would prolong his life. He believed that as his job was done, living longer wouldn't make any sense. His wish was to be cremated: no grave or shrine for him.

WORK IS WORK – PLEASURE IS PLEASURE

But sometimes work is more than pleasure: it's all up to us, what our Mind tells us. Ordinary routines can be enjoyed because they can lead to extraordinary results. Medical staff during the pandemic and their boring, everyday duties in hospitals in every country have been very much appreciated – they are our heroes! Not all is 'boring', you can notice happy moments and it will keep you going – it's all about the right attitude.

It takes courage, it takes strength, it takes wisdom!

GREAT AUTHORS

What do you think about great authors? Was Shakespeare's life very exciting? Writing his books without the help of a computer; the long, lonely hours... He knew and believed in his work. His aim was for his plays to be performed to stir, engage and move people.

QUIET MIND

A quiet mind is great happiness and great beauty. Whatever life throws at you, try to take it quietly and hold it lightly. Accept it – its 2000 year old wisdom from Marcus Aurelius. A quiet mind will find its way of dealing with anything and everything. Avoid courts and lawyers and litigations.

DEATH MAKES A PERSON

When a good person dies, we want to know about them and treasure what they did for humanity. It will enrich our lives and make us happy. That's how many people felt very recently about the Duke of Edinburgh, a person of great dignity. When a 'bad' person dies we are relieved – one 'evil' less!

DON'T JUST BE YOURSELF

There are beautiful flowers that are scentless, and beautiful-looking people who are unlovable. Don't just be 'yourself' – be someone a bit nicer. A kind word opens iron gates.

PRAISE LOUDLY, BLAME SOFTLY

Praise loudly, blame softly, we're told. Don't judge! Is it right? There are situations in life when we need to 'judge' in order to support life. How can we make any positive changes if we don't take notice of people's wrongdoings? Recently we have been angry about violence against women who have been abducted and murdered. Should we not judge 'evil'?

CHILDREN

Praising and blaming when it comes to children and young people is a different story! Children are learning how to cope with life and people. They need our guidance and good role models. As adults, as parents, we are partly responsible for our young people's behaviour. It's great to remember that we need to praise loudly, for others to learn. Blaming should be done in private and not in front of the whole class – it shouldn't be robbing our children of their dignity. Everything in moderation, not everything in life is black and white. Grey areas can be very important.

A THANKFUL PERSON

A thankful person is thankful under all circumstances. A complaining soul loves complaining. Some people just like to be miserable.

STANDING UP TO HUMAN EVIL

Standing up to human evil is our moral duty. Anybody who has suffered injustice, or who has been the victim of violence and abuse, or any other form of evil, should talk about it in order to let the world know what is happening around us. This way potential victims can be protected. We ought to fight human evil with determination and precision, to let abusers know that we are not afraid of them.

BEING MAD

There's a pleasure, sure, in being mad, which none but the mad know. Every 'fool' has his 'brain'. He knows what he wants and how to get it. And he doesn't care whom he hurts. Mad people are very dangerous: stupidity has no pain. Even God can't deal with madness.

PSYCHOPATHS AND PRETENCE

Psychopaths look good and may exhibit warm emotions and the appearance of being loving, but they experience feelings of: anger, resentment, envy, jealousy, revenge. Some will also have murderous tendencies. When they are with people they wear a mask of normality. They're very good at pretending and very often get away with it. But not for too long. When they betray you, you will get to know their true colours.

HOPE

We need hope to stay alive, even 'silly' hope. but still hope. When things go wrong in our life, there's only so much we can do. Wisdom tells us – *wait and hope*. it gives us some peace. If you lose hope, you have nothing left.

CHARACTER

We develop character in the face of suffering and danger. How can a little boy learn how to be brave if his life is always comfortable? Learning how to be brave must have something of value. No value, no meaning. To be brave doesn't mean to be silly and take unnecessary risks just to impress!

PARENTS

Do parents need to earn the right to be a parent? As parents, do we know our responsibilities? You need training in order to be a plumber. Children need our attention and love. They must *feel* being loved, to tell a child 'Dad loves you' is not enough!

It's easier to be a parent in a smaller family, we can share our time and love with all our children equally, no favourites. We love all our children unconditionally and equally. A child doesn't have to earn their parents' love. Our children's achievements are the proverbial icing on a cake. Abused, neglected children may grow into angry adults and crave revenge. Children mustn't be blamed for their parents' ignorance or lack of responsibility.

NOT EVERYBODY IS HAPPY IN THEIR WORK

Sometimes workmates make your life miserable and at times like this a good manager can be vital. A good manager is a wise manager, who understands the complexity of human nature and knows how to reason with people. People are good at heart. Some of us are just misguided. We spend many hours of our life at work – and we need to enjoy it. After the working week the weekend has its special meaning. Unemployed people can't be happy!

IT'S A BEAUTIFUL WORLD

Work hard, live your life, laugh often, love much, stay alive. It's a beautiful world, even if it's not perfect.

TELLING LIES

Telling lies is one of the symptoms and one of the causes of evil. Liars take us for idiots. They expect us to believe them. Psychopaths are very good liars. They think they are the winners, smarter than the rest of us. Children may tell lies because they might be afraid of adults. For the child of an alcoholic parent, telling lies is a way to survive. Grown up liars are cowards. They are also their own enemies: can they trust others, or do they assume that everyone is a liar?

SURVIVING DEFEAT

You have to learn to survive defeat – that's when you develop your character.

BE YOURSELF

Just be who you are. Some people will love you for who you are. Some people will love you for what you can do for them, and some won't like you at all. So what! A who cares attitude is good.

A NICE PERSON?

The person who is nice to you and not nice to a waiter is not a nice person. He was raised to be charming, not sincere.

CHEERFULNESS

My religion of life is to be always cheerful. Apparently cheerfulness is good for our immune system. Cheerful people live longer. Try to pretend that you are cheerful. After some hours of pretending you will really be cheerful. It will help you face the world.

IDEAL CIRCUMSTANCES

Do ideal circumstances exist? Can you plan your life the way it would suit you? We can have some control, but only some! The rest . . . we can only hope. If something is really very important to you, for example, having a baby, find the courage to take a reasonable risk and don't wait for ideal circumstances – just hope that you will somehow manage to cope.

SELF-CONFIDENCE

You have a very important meeting next week and you're dreading it. An important key to self-confidence is preparation. You have to do your research, to know what you will be talking about. You can practise your speech in front of the mirror, looking at your watch to see how long it takes. You will know how to answer tricky questions because you have the confidence to do so.

LOSS

Things and money can be replaced. The important thing is that you are not hurt. You lose, you gain, that's life, accept it. I lost my purse one day and was angry with myself. My lovely friend cheered me up saying, 'Just think that a good person found your purse and she desperately needed it. She's smiling, let it make you happy. It's only money – paper notes! Next time take good care of your purse. Keep it safe!'

ASTROLOGY

Horoscopes – do you read them regularly or only when the prediction sounds kind? Would you like to know what Shakespeare has to say:

'Men at some time are masters of their fates;
The fault, dear Brutus, is not in our stars,
But in ourselves, that we are underlings.'

ACCEPTING FAVOURS

Have you got the courage to refuse favours? Try to learn it and practise it. Favours always have expectations. People will give and then expect to get something back in return. Do you need that? The only special thing is giving for the sake of giving. Try to be wise next time. Have modest doubts about people's motives. You are in control. It's easy to say. *'No thank you!'*

LENDING MONEY

Sometimes you lend some money to a friend you trust. When it comes to money, trust no one, even a friend. Money has weird power. If you lose money, say to yourself: it was worth it, you did learn who your friend was. Some wisdom about it from Aesop: Don't be angry, disappointed, tell your friends: 'Keep the money, it's my gift for you.' That's the good way to forget about the money. A wise man also says, 'Lend only as much as you can afford to lose.'

HUMILITY

Find the courage to say: unfortunately, I don't know the answer, could anyone help me? Humility is a very special gift. Use your speech as the chance to shine. Act as if it was impossible to fail. You will be OK.

JOY IN LIVING

Taking joy in living is woman's best cosmetic. I do feel sad to see young girls and young women with good complexions, wearing foundation masks. When you choose the wrong shade, you might look like an orange. It's OK in the evening, in artificial light, but during the day it does look sad. Cosmetic companies make big money, playing on our insecurities.

DATING

Dating is like a box of chocolates. Sometimes you get something weird but keep going on dates and one day you will meet your prince or princess. You have to believe it and have hope. Good people are looking for love, just like you are!

VIOLENCE AND CRIME

Education is the only answer.

+ There's no sense in fighting, it's ridiculous.
+ You can be hurt or your enemy can be hurt.
+ One of you can be dead.
+ You can't benefit from hurting others.

You can also find humour in it. When two drunk men fight they can't even enjoy it – they will be surprised to end up in a hospital.

DON'T CRY FOR THINGS

Things won't cry for you. The robbed person who smiles steals something from the thief. Don't dwell too much on what you have lost.

STEALING

For children, it's often an angry act – they may do it for attention. If parents don't pay attention to their young child's emotional needs, the child might be angry. Stealing is a good way of getting it. It can even give the child a chance for a new, better life.

MONEY SHOULD BE OUR SLAVE

Let me share with you very precious wisdom from Benjamin Disraeli, the nineteenth-century British prime minister. Money should be our slave, not master. Don't allow money to be in control of your life. I don't count anybody's money. I'm pleased for wealthy people. Some of them are great philanthropists, supporting good causes. Money can't buy us happiness, you don't know who your real friends are. Wise thinking can be very liberating!

JUSTICE AND INJUSTICE

Injustice is as old as the world. No justice in and out of court. Crooks who could afford expensive lawyers walk away free. So unfair, we have to accept that money 'talks', nothing new! Human capacity for evil is scary. People will do anything for money when the price is right. Abraham Lincoln – a lawyer before becoming President – convinced people that litigation in court is a bad idea. Out of court agreement, he argued, is much better and saves you a lot of pain.

COURT JUDGES

Are they all well prepared for their job? There's no justice without Wisdom; there's no justice without Compassion. Do they understand human nature well enough? The air in the court can be very scary: being innocent is not good enough! When things are getting complicated with not much hope for you, choose Wisdom to surrender. Try to see the big picture of things. Never sell your house to pay greedy lawyers. Nobody ever promised us that life will be fair. *Be wise.*

INJUSTICE IN THE FAMILY

Injustice in the family is where parents favour some of their children over others, saying, 'Why can't you be like your brother or sister?' A very sensitive child will take the painful childhood memories with them to their adulthood and hate their parents. It can affect the child's life very badly. Have the courage to confront your parents about it. You're no longer a little child afraid of your parents. Say exactly how you feel. You're allowed to be angry. We don't have to 'love' our parents – respect is enough. Let's teach our children about humanity and moral greatness. Let's teach them Wisdom.

A WISE WOMAN

There's nothing like having a good, wise woman, her mind and heart, not only her looks. Sadly, for some men, a pretty woman is like a shiny toy to a little boy. Grow up, boys, *be wise!*

CARING FATHER

A caring father will tell his son: love is a beautiful thing, so is marriage. But take time to commit yourself, think well, ask questions, talk. Good looks, love, sex are not enough.

TRUTH

You have your world, I've got mine. You have your truth, I've got mine. Try to remember not to allow anyone to convince you about their truth. You have a choice to be yourself, and as long as you don't hurt anyone with your choices, everything else is OK. Be tolerant of people who think differently. It's their right too!

A SMILE THROUGH TEARS

A smile through tears is a human miracle. When you're in pain for any reason and manage a smile, it's a very special smile. It's about the resilience of human spirit and can be a great comfort for people around you. It's also about hope for a better tomorrow.

LEARNING ABOUT PEOPLE

The more I learn about humans, the more I love my cat.

INDIFFERENCE TO HUMAN SUFFERING

It may not wreck someone's life at any turn but it will destroy them with a kind of dry rot in the long run. I read about a rich man who was living with guilt – not taking care of his poor mother when she was ill. It was so painful for him, he committed suicide.

LINCOLN, EINSTEIN AND HUMILITY

The Oxford English Dictionary's definition of humility is 'humble attitude of mind'. It's about modesty. Big people are never big, small people are never small – they pretend to be big. Abraham Lincoln, the great American President, is a wonderful symbol of humility. Einstein, the greatest scientist ever, is the other one. I would advise you to learn more about the two men and their lives. You will love it. Young people desperately need good role models.

Truly great people are wise and humble

SEEK THE GOOD IN PEOPLE

God created all things – including all human beings. So seek the good in people. It will make your life so much easier, and so much happier. Resentment hurts and is no good for your health either. Understanding others is half way to forgiveness of their bad behaviour. Accept them for what they are. Live and let live – as simple as that!

RACISM AND IGNORANCE

Racism is nothing more than ignorance. It's hard for us to accept people who are different from us in any way. People are good or bad, it has nothing to do with their skin colour or their race. Let's raise our new generation guiding young people with love and logic. Teach them about Wisdom as early as possible. School ought to play a big role in it. We need to trust human nature.

IT'S NEVER TOO LATE

It's never too late to change your mind.
The last word has not been spoken,
The last sentence has not been written,
The final verdict is not in.
It's never too late to change my mind or direction,
To say NO to past and YES to future,
To offer remorse and ask for forgiveness.
It's never too late to start over again,
To feel again, to love again, to hope again.

MIGRANTS AND FOREIGNERS

Please read this message and I hope you'll have some compassion for migrants to our country.

Sweet nostalgia about my motherland, land that gave birth to me. The air of your native land is sweet, the simplicity and sweetness of my Polish childhood, even now, make my life beautiful. I do remember the beautiful smell of jasmin in my neighbour's garden in June. I do remember the taste of a blueberry soup in summer and the sound of my father's laughter. I love beautiful England very much. It accepted me without questions all those 55 years ago. I love true Britishness – it gave me a chance to flourish. I pray in Polish (can God understand English – how can I know?). Please try to be kind to people like my mother, they are more than just 'bloody foreigners'. Thank you.

A KIND OF DEATH

To be alive but forgotten or neglected or denied – is that not a kind of life? Let us now praise the minds and hearts of our famous fathers. Aesop, who lived 2,500 years ago, the wisest man, is still alive to me. His *Aesop's Fables* is my most precious book.

WHEN YOU'RE IN A HOLE

When you're in a hole, stop digging. When we're in trouble, when some lies were already said, we mustn't make the situation any worse by adding any more lies! We need to find the Courage to be Wise, to apologise and put an end to the whole mess. And one more thing: we should learn some Wisdom from experience!

THE REVOLVING YEAR

'Winter has come and gone. But grief returns with the revolving year.'

Percy Bysshe Shelley, *Adonais*

MAN LIVES BY PAIN

It's so easy to remember our suffering. There are painful moments in our lives that could never be forgotten no matter how hard we try. Time will soften the pain a little, that's all, painful memories will stay for ever. Have self-compassion, be kind to yourself and to your memories, embrace them and manage a gentle smile.

LETTING GO

Love is proved in letting go, wish him well. One day he'll probably regret leaving you. One day he'll realise how special you are. And don't bad-mouth him to your children. They will feel sad, thinking: if he's rubbish, we're rubbish too, he's our father. Children desperately need love from both parents. Never use your children as 'weapons' to punish your ex and let them see their Dad as often as possible. We don't own our children, they belong to both parents.

ANGER, HURT AND GUILT

Behind anger, hurt or guilt hide. Angry women cry and criticise. Don't repress your feelings with drugs, alcohol, shopping, sex. Just talk, and talk about it with people who wish you well. It will never go away for good, but you will start feeling better.

LIFE'S DIFFICULTIES

Our difficulties in life don't have to be always negative. For example, you lost your job and are very upset about it. Some difficulties can be a blessing in disguise. Your next job can be much better than the one you had! Your second husband can be better than the one who left you. Don't be afraid of change. Some of our difficulties can be purely emotional, and we can be in control of our thoughts. Think with your Mind as well as your heart. Learn to laugh at yourself and try to see the funny side of things. It does help!

A SUICIDE NOTE

The following suicide note was written by a young man:

> 'Easy to die. Love to my mother.
> Everything ends somewhere.'

Terriby sad, but is our right to keep alive people who can't cope with everyday life for any reason. Who has the answer to that? It's OK to be strong. It's OK to be weak, Saving somebody's life is not enough. The person needs constant support. Could you manage that? What about your family – they need you in the first place!

LIFE CAN BE COMIC OR TRAGIC

It depends on our attitude. Some men like 'difficult' women. Some women like 'difficult' men. They like the excitement of fighting and making up, they think it's passion! A young attractive wife told me the other day, 'He's good, he's very good, he makes me feel sick.' I feel sad for her husband. Can you win?

PUNISHMENT

I like this simple observation: parents, teachers, judges, policemen have the power to punish a teenager, nothing else. Children need loving guidance, not punishment. They need love. Our children are often neglected by our society and by families. We fling them out into a void and leave them there. Many unhappy teenagers will tell you anger, 'I didn't want to be born.'

TACT

'She's tactful', people will say. The Oxford English Dictionary definition of tact is: 'sensitivity and skill in dealing with others'. A tactful person won't boast about their fantastic holiday in Spain to someone who can't afford holidays. Even more tactless would be talking about your perfect family life to a single parent, mother or father. Empathy is a great gift.

BE GOOD TO YOURSELF

You're in a bad place at the moment: anguish and despair can be very painful. It's obvious: your mind and your body need rest – let's call it rest – cure, not medication. Your mind, your nervous system are tired. Try to close the door on the world, nothing to hear, not reading rubbish on the internet, nothing to think about – just perfect silence – and drinking water. Your body and mind will recover. Be good to yourself.

MUMMY'S BOY

A young boy, obsessed with his mother, can grow into an adult depending too much on women. 'Mummy's boy' will one day want to marry a woman exactly like his mother. Let's try to raise our young boys to be strong and independent.

RECEIVING FROM OTHERS

Receiving from others is an act of humility. It recognises others' dignity and worth. Allowing others to serve us shows our respect and love for the giver.

SEX

In our crazy, modern culture sex is everywhere. This is sexy, that is sexy, sex sells. Would you agree that it's a bit sick? Sex is the oldest 'magic' in the world, and we're gullible about it. Sex is the strongest instinct that plays on simple human weakness and can cause a lot of pain to us all in the long run. Boy George, the signer, was 'brave' to share publicly on TV: 'I prefer a good cup of tea to sex.'

CONFESSIONS OF A MAN

A man confessed: 'I felt used and abused by women. They expected dinner dates in flashy restaurants and sex in hotel rooms later, even if I wasn't in the mood for it. I was a fool.'

TRAUMATISED GENIUS

So many of them around and so painful. John Lennon was one of them. His life let him down. His mother died when he was very young and he had emotional problems. He had fame and money, but he needed peace in his mind and heart. He was a very sensitive, unhappy man. Famous people, overwhelmed by their fame, very often question it and suffer emotionally.

A GAME OF FOOLS

Our young people need to learn that fame is a game of fools, an empty bubble. They need to believe in themselves and be content with who they are! Our minds can play scary tricks on us. John Lennon paid a big price for his fame – assassinated by a fan at the age of 40! How ironic, how very sad!

SCARED OF FAME

I was happy to read about a young, promising singer who became scared of fame and stopped singing, saying: 'I prefer to go and visit my mum.' Charlie Chaplin was scared of crowds who came to see him at a train station during his travels. What kind of life is that? Wisdom is the only thing that can 'save' us.

CREATING OUR OWN PAIN

It happens when we are jealous, being negative, judging and resenting others. Other people's lives are not our business. The less you know, the less you worry about. Pain created by yourself won't need to last long. It needs a healthy attitude, nothing else. We are in control of our minds and we need Wisdom.

THERE'S NO POINT IN FIGHTING

Talking and sorting things out is easier and safer. It takes a strong person to walk away from a fight. We need to teach our young children about it! The funny side of it? When two drunk, angry men fight, they are scared to wake up in a hospital the next morning!

GUILT CAN BE PAINFUL

Guilt can be a painful, dangerous emotion and destroy our life. Sometimes our guilt is imaginary. We convince ourselves that it was our fault. A sensitive person will torture himself for no obvious reason. I know a man who blames himself for his young son's death and can't forgive himself for it. He needs to take control of his thinking. He needs to ask for help. It takes courage, but it can be done.

REAL GUILT

Real guilt, when you intentionally hurt someone, is another, serious matter. It can drive you crazy or even destroy you. You need to apologise, from your heart, and ask for forgiveness, as soon as you can, or it might be too late – a person might die. Do it today!

AFRAID OF DYING

Are you afraid of dying? I think we all are, especially when we grow a lot older. Our mortality is so obvious – we will all die one day. I like what Shakespeare had to say about death:

> 'A coward dies a thousand times before his death, but the valiant taste of death but once. It seems to me most strange that men should fear, seeing that death, a necessary end, will come when it will come.'

> '... and our little life
> Is rounded with a sleep.'

A WIDOW

A widow, when asked, how she was coping with the loss of her husband, replied: 'I'm OK, because the last thing I had a chance to tell him was: "I love you!"'

GIVING IS LIVING

If you stop wanting to give, you stop living. We can give money, our time, great advice etc. We are here on Earth for others:

Giving for the sake of giving
Is happiness, not duty.

OUR SOULS

The body can't live without food. The soul can't live without meaning. Life without meaning can be a torture, just eating and sleeping. Find something interesting to do and do it. Don't worry about anything else or anybody, including your family. Happiness is doing what you love doing!

BE KIND TO YOUR ENEMY

'Be kind to your enemy, nothing can upset them more,' said Oscar Wilde. Nelson Mandela was always kind to his enemies and treated them like his old, best friends. He called everybody 'darling'. While in prison, he learned his enemies' language. He tried to 'kill' them with his kindness. So much better than resentment.

CRYING

Crying washes your pain and anxiety away and makes room for something new. Only strong men weep. We all need to suffer a little to appreciate happiness later. Every cloud has a silver lining.

ATTRACTIVE WOMEN

Not all men go for attractive women. Some men value women's minds and character. Looks go, character stays. Benjamin Franklin famously wrote an 'Ode to His Wife', praising her for her character, not her looks.

BEING YOURSELF IS AN ART

Style is confidence and easiness, feeling good about yourself.

PARENTS' LOVE

Our parents' love and prayers follow us wherever we are. Parents want to protect us from the unkind world and their prayers give us a lot of comfort.

TALENTS AND GOOD LOOKS

Talents and good looks are not an achievement, they are God given. Be humbled! Big people are never big; small people are never small; they pretend to be 'big'.

FORGIVENESS IS A CHOICE

You will never be ready to forgive. Why? Because it's so difficult to forget our pain. We forgive in our mind, we know it makes sense, but our heart doesn't always listen. Just choose to forgive and do it, and enjoy a resentment-free life. Be good to yourself.

SARCASM

Sarcasm can hurt – there's some truth in every joke. Saying 'I was only joking' isn't good enough. Think before you open your mouth; once you've said it, you can't take it back. Words can be a cruel drug used by mankind.

PAIN IS HIDDEN

Pain is hidden in every decision we make. Pain and happiness are twin sisters. You were happy to get married, you are sad now being on your own. Our beautiful babies give us so much happiness, but they also have the power to hurt us later. You were happy when your affair lasted – you're sad now because your lover left you.

MARRIAGE

Marriage can be a very precious gift to two people, to appreciate and enjoy. President George Washington had a very happy marriage. His advice to a friend was: 'Marry anyway. If you're lucky you will be happy. If not, you will become a philosopher.'

STICKS AND STONES...

What does it matter what you say about people? What does it matter what they say about you? Happiness is good health and short memory, just forget it, as simple as that! It's a different matter when evil people try to destroy you, intentionally! You need to defend your reputation. You have to take it seriously.

FOOL THE PEOPLE

'You can fool all of the people some of the time, and some of the people all of the time but you can't fool all of the people, all of the time.'

Abraham Lincoln

TRUST STRANGERS

It's easier to trust strangers because they have never deceived us.

VILLAINY

'One may smile and smile and be a villain.'

William Shakespeare, *Hamlet*

PEACEFULNESS

Peacefulness follows any decision, even the wrong one. It's hard to decide sometimes what to do, what's right or wrong, good or bad. Once we decide, we're at peace and hope for the best. Life gives no guarantees!

FAST WALKING

It is impossible to walk rapidly and be unhappy. Why? Our mind focuses on walking, to avoid tripping over, and doesn't have the time to think silly, depressive thoughts. Our mind is busy.

HOW TO CHEER YOURSELF UP

The best way to cheer yourself up is to try to cheer someone else up! When we're busy with someone else's pain, we don't have the time to think about our problems.

LOOK CLOSELY

There's so much beauty around us, but we are too 'busy' to notice it. Pay close attention to anything, even a blade of grass; it becomes a mysterious, awesome, magnificent world in itself.

ARGUMENTS FOR DIVORCE

In every marriage, more than a week old, there are arguments for divorce. The Wisdom is to find, and continue to find, grounds for marriage.

WISDOM IS PATIENT

Sometimes, when we ignore our neighbour's complaint for some time, they might forget about it.

DO NOTHING

'To do nothing is sometimes good remedy.'

Hippocrates

THE WORLD IS A COMEDY

The world is a comedy to those wise thoughts and a tragedy to those who think with painful emotions. Thinking is a part of Wisdom. Wise people will think and laugh at themselves and at life. Our existence can be absurd sometimes.

PEOPLE WILL FORGET

People will forget what you said, what you did, but never forget how you made them feel. It reminds me of an incident when I asked to see the manager over a problem I was having in a store. I'm glad I did: he was a man who understood 'emotional intuition'. He knew how to talk to me and I will always value his kindness.

SAD BUT REAL OBSERVATION

'Anybody can sympathise with the suffering of a friend but it requires a very fine nature to sympathise with a friend's success,' a wise woman said. Your friends are happy for you when you do well, but not too well. People often prefer to hear sad news... Human nature is very complex.

NOTHING IS AS GOOD AS IT SEEMS BEFOREHAND

Sometimes we think we like something. Once we buy it and bring it home, we no longer like it and can be irritated by it and angry with ourselves. Our minds do play tricks on us. Be in control!

NOT EVERY EXPERT IS AN EXPERT

When experts all agree, they may all be mistaken. Doesn't matter how many people agree on something, they all could be wrong. Eighty years ago, the whole of Germany supported Hitler, they trusted him, he was a great leader. Nobody knew him well enough to address his insecurities and mental problems and a great tragedy happened. Have modest doubt about everything in life.

IT TAKES COURAGE TO MAKE A FOOL OF YOURSELF

Life is difficult enough to be taken seriously all the time. Try to have 'so what' attitude and don't worry about everything all the time. Act humbly and feel confident. You know who you are and those who know us, know us better and those who don't, don't matter. Take everything with a pinch of salt.

THE KEY TO FAILURE

The key to failure is to try to please everybody. Start pleasing yourself. Be positively selfish.

HAVING TOO MUCH

Some people are ruined by having too much of everything: money, power, fame. Enjoy little things, like being able to think clearly, to feel the rain, to laugh and to love, to be a good human being. Don't envy anybody anything!

FATHERS

Men need to understand their self-worth and value what they mean to their daughters. Absence of a father can badly affect a little girl and a young woman. Father is the first man who loves her, or is supposed to love her. How will she understand what man's love should be about and what to expect from her future husband?

REMORSE

Deep regret for our wrongdoings is one of the most painful emotions that mentally healthy people will experience. Sort things out with people in your life and apologise. Sociopaths may not experience remorse or feel any emotion, not even when they are sentenced to death.

FAKE INTEREST

Don't have any fake interest in anything; don't pretend just to please someone. Have the courage to say *no thankyou* to gifts and favours, and ignore TV commercials. People will respect you for that. Only sometimes can fake interest be forgiven, when we need to avoid hurting someone very important in our lives.

FOLLOWING OTHERS

If you don't agree with other people's behaviour, try always to believe that you're made for better things. Don't follow fools – listen to advice, but the final decision should be yours and only yours.

Be brave to be wise!

WE'RE ALL A BIT MAD

Some of us realise it. No one is perfect, we're only human. We come from different backgrounds. We all have one thing in common: we all want to be happy and not suffer.

HIS LITTLE THINGS

He was real, not perfect. He was human – a good man with a few bad habits. His legacy is special and we forgive him 'his little things'. We love our not perfect parents. Why? Because we need to love them – we need their love, even if it's not perfect.

TAKE THINGS SLOWLY

Learn to take things slowly, seriously, but hold them lightly. Good things take time. Wisdom is patient. Don't stamp like an impatient racehorse. *There's time for everything – wait and hope.*

EYES THAT WEPT

Eyes that wept can see things more clearly. Any trauma teaches us something about life and human nature. Comfortable life could be boring. Don't avoid little sufferings: they are character building and help you understand others.

POWER OF HUMOUR AND STORYTELLING

Humour helps us understand the silliness around us. Funny stories are a great gift. If children love a funny story, they will remember it for long and the moral in it.

YOU CAN'T HAVE TWO LIVES, JUST ONE

You can't have a wife and a mistress. You have to reject her altogether, not hurt your family. You can't serve two masters, you need to be on firm ground.

PERSONAL AND PROFESSIONAL INTEGRITY

Someone with personal and professional integrity will have knowledge in their head and wisdom in their heart. It's amazing what they can do!

TEACHERS

At my school we were taught how to learn, how to think and reason, how to love, how to care. School is about more than just ABC. A teacher affects eternity, he shapes young minds. We need *enthusiastic teachers!*

FAME

Scandal brought him 'sick' success and fame. People are desperate for any kind of fame. Even 'fifteen minutes' fame will do. Some go to extremes, being famous as a criminal. People are gullible. They don't think.

BUYING A HOUSE

Choose a neighbour first! We need good, kind people around us. Have you heard of 'neighbours from Hell?'

FAMILY

Family can be a dangerous institution. More siblings, more trouble. What can we do? We need our family, we need to belong.

YOUR UNIQUE GIFT

Every one of us has a unique gift. Have you found yours? Take time to do it, it will be a golden moment when you know what you're good at!

TOLERATING BAD BEHAVIOUR

I am a fool, a bloody idiot, to tolerate his bad behaviour for so long. I need courage to stand up to 'human evil'. I don't need to suffer.

DETERMINATION

To achieve something in life you need determination and a strong will. Talking about it is not enough. 'Good talkers are bad doers.' You have to believe in yourself so others will believe in you as well.

QUALITIES OF A GOOD PERSON

Gentle, honest, dependable, unselfish, solid, upright, etc. We need a kinder, wiser society. Why are we so angry all the time? Don't fear anyone enough to be afraid to tell him the truth. *Be brave to confront crooks!*

THE DAY THE CHILD LEARNS

The day the child learns that adults are not perfect, he becomes an adolescent. The day he forgives them, he becomes an adult. The day he forgives himself he becomes wise.

PARENTS' LEGACY

Parents' legacy has to be Wisdom and understanding of human nature. Our children need to grow wise and strong, to be ready to face an unkind world.

WRINKLES

Wrinkles mean that you laughed, grey hair that you cared, scars that you lived. You don't need any alterations or plastic surgery. Just be as beautiful as you are. When you're old, would you like to have a young face on your shoulders? Wouldn't that be very strange?

LYING AND COURAGE

She was telling lies to defend her reputation. She knew she was wrong: she wanted to cover up something. Truth is simple, but often painful. You need courage, liars are cowards!

WISDOM AND REASON

It's Wisdom and reason that take away cares, and not going on an expensive holiday. When you're unhappy, you have to share it with people you trust, and you both can do some thinking and reasoning. A holiday can be pleasant but your pain will still be there when you're back at home.

THE EARTH LAUGHS

The Earth laughs in flowers. The beauty of flowers gives us hope: not everything in the world can be bad.

A FOOLISH THING

Even if fifty million people say a foolish thing, it's still a foolish thing. Trust your own instinct.

REVENGE AND FORGIVENESS

There's no revenge as complete as forgiveness.

FREEDOM OF SPEECH

I disagree and disapprove of what you say, but will defend your right to say it!

GENIUS

I don't want to be a genius. I have enough problems just trying to be a man.

THE WICKED

The wicked are always surprised to find out that the wicked can be clever.

GOSSIP

Gossip doesn't need to be false to be evil. There's a lot of truth shouldn't be passed around. Whoever gossips with you will gossip about you.

IF YOU DON'T KNOW WHAT TO SAY...

If you don't know what to say, just be there to hold your friend's hand. It will make a difference.

ENTHUSIASM

Being enthusiastic about things brings happiness. We can learn that from our children.

HELL

Hell is other people. Keep away from shady characters: you owe them nothing.

LISTEN CAREFULLY

Listen carefully to what people say. A person who is 'brutally honest' often enjoys their brutality more than anything.

DON'T CALL SOMEONE HONEST...

... just because they have never had the chance to steal.

IMAGINATION

'Imagination is more important than knowledge.' (Einstein) If you can imagine yourself being a teacher or a doctor, you can be a teacher and you can be a doctor. The choice is yours.

INDIFFERENCE

The opposite of love is not hate, it's indifference.

IGNORANCE

Life gets harder the smarter you get and the more you know. The less you know the less you worry about. Ignorance can be bliss. Don't watch too much TV.

KINDNESS

We are made kind by being kind. Women need kindness more than love. When one human being is kind to another, it is a very deep matter.

KNOWLEDGE VERSUS WISDOM

To know is not to be wise. To know how to use your knowledge is Wisdom.

BE KIND TO YOURSELF

It's easy to say: Sorry, I don't know.

LYING AND BELIEVING

Can you believe anyone else if you're a liar?

DEFINITION OF A HUMAN

A human is an ungrateful animal on two feet.

POLITENESS

Treat everyone with politeness, even those who are rude to you, not because they're nice but because you are.

RUDENESS

Rudeness is the weak person's imitation of strength.

BE HAPPY

Nobody really cares if you're miserable so you might as well be happy!

SOCIAL GRACE

Allowing a small mistake to pass without comment is a social grace.

MONEY

With money in your pocket you're wise, you're handsome and you sing well too!

OWING NOTHING

The person who owes nothing is rich. Don't borrow money unless you really have to.

THE WORLD OWES YOU NOTHING

Don't go around saying the world owes you a living. The world owes you nothing: it was here first.

WAIT AND HOPE

All great human Wisdom is in two words: wait and hope.

POWER

If you want to test a person's character, give them power; they might get drunk on it!

PRISON

Wow, look at the toilets, and just inches from your bed. What a luxury. Keep away from prison – it's worse than murder!

SOLVING A PROBLEM

The next best thing to solving a problem is finding some humour in it, for example: 'Don't worry about it too much, my friend. In 80 years, we will both definitely be dead.'

THE NEED TO BE RIGHT

The need to be always right is the sign of a vulgar mind.

MAKE YOUR LIFE A MISSION

Make your life a mission, do something for humanity in a practical way.

KNOWING

The one who knows others is learned; the one who knows themself is wise.

THE NEED FOR THINGS

Even bargains cost money; we don't need more things. We need Wisdom.

THE BEST THINGS IN LIFE

The best things in life are not things, they can't love you back.

STUPIDITY

It's too bad that stupidity isn't painful.

THE SAD PART OF SUCCESS

The sad part of success is to try to find someone who would be happy for you.

LOVING AND LEAVING

If someone leaves you, it doesn't mean they don't love you. They look after their own interests. They love themself more.

UNHAPPY MARRIAGES

Don't tell people about your unhappy marriage. One half won't care and the other half will be glad!

SITTING AND THINKING

Sometimes I just sit and think.
Sometimes I just sit.
Thinking is harder work than hard work.

NOTHING LASTS

Nothing very, very good and nothing very, very bad lasts for very, very long. Relax and cheer up!

TIGHT SHOES

If you want to forget about your trouble, wear tight shoes.

TRUST

'I trust you' means more than 'I love you'. You can love many but trust only a few.

TRUST IN ALLAH...

...but tie your camel.

CONDEMNATION

One should never condemn what one can't understand.

UNDERSTANDING

You don't really understand something, unless you can explain it to your grandma.

THE WISDOM OF BENJAMIN FRANKLIN

People will accept your idea much more rapidly if you tell them Benjamin Franklin said it first.

ORDINARY ROUTINES

Ordinary routines can be boring, but they can lead to something extraordinary. We need to accept the fact that life is about repetition and enjoy it. You can't have excitement all the time. Boring routines: raising a baby, boring studies when you are at school or college. One day you will have your diploma and your 'baby' will be older and looking after themself. It goes the same for many different things. Wisdom is patient – enjoy your boring routines.

ETHICALLY POSITIVE BEHAVIOUR

Ethically positive behaviour brings happiness and more meaning to our life. We can learn to cope with suffering and prevent some suffering.

BAD BEHAVIOUR

Scientists, lawyers, judges and policemen can help us see that our behaviour is bad and punish us for it. They can't teach us how we ought to act in a moral sense. That is the responsibility of parents and teachers at school.

REASONS FOR OPTIMISM

There's still much in our crazy modern life to be optimistic about. Countless people show concern for others. People are happy to help during natural disasters.

THE MOST IMPORTANT QUESTION

Is he a good human being? is more important than anything else.

SAD THINGS IN OUR WORLD

Crime, violence, drugs, divorce, suicide, etc. It's everybody's responsibility to do something, to make our world a better place. We need to understand what's happening. The lives of many criminal are lonely and lacking in love.

KEEP SMILING

Human beings' ability to smile is one of the most beautiful characteristics. Animals can't smile. I'm touched when a stranger smiles at me. I smile back out of appreciation for their kindness.

PEOPLE ARE LOVING BY NATURE

We all share the capacity for loving kindness. We tend to reserve it for those close to us.

THERE'S GOOD AND BAD IN EVERYONE

We're capable of cruelty and hatred. Two sides of human potential. Human nature can be aggressive: good news is not news. An ethical act is a non-harming act. We need empathy and compassion. Objects don't have feelings. Will your wardrobe give a hug? When we start talking to strangers, our shyness, insecurity disappear. We become more confident and worry less. There's nothing more beautiful than the heart of a volunteer.

WHEN I MEET A STRANGER

I know he looks the same as me, has the same desire to be happy and to avoid suffering. I can talk to him freely about everything including my feelings. I enjoy talking to a stranger who will listen and share. Not all people that we meet will be nice. We can sense it and trust our instinct. Acting out of concern for others can give us peace in our hearts, and we bring peace to everyone with whom we associate.

PEACE TO THE WORLD

We can bring peace to our family, friends, workplace, to the community, and so to the world. What can be more important? Teaching to value love and compassion – we owe it to our children.

AFFLICTING EMOTIONS

Anger, pride, lust, greed, envy etc. can be very strong. If we do nothing about them they can lead us to the extremes of madness, or even suicide itself. Murder, scandal, deceit, all have their origin in afflicting emotions.

ILL TREATMENT

Some not very nice people will believe of some others that they deserve ill treatment. A cruel person will suppress their kind feelings and will do the bad thing. Intentionally hurting people or animals is a crime. One day, close to his death, a cruel man might become lonely, anxious, full of dread and suspicion of everyone. His conscience might trouble him – not an easy way to die.

GOOD REPUTATION

Good reputation is a source of happiness. People who care about others are much respected. When they die, many mourn and regret their passing.

NEGATIVE EMOTIONS

Negative emotions can also ruin our health. Anger, for example, can give us high blood pressure, sleeplessness. Cheerful people live longer.

LUST

Relationships founded primarily on sexual attraction are almost always unstable and lead to disaster.

PROBLEMS WITH WOMEN

If you are emotional with women you will always have problems with them. You do everything to make them happy, at any price, even if that makes you vulnerable to them. It has something to do with your relationship with your mother.

INSECURITY

I was so insecure, so scared of loss, so afraid to be alone. I was moving from one person to another. That's all my mother ever did, moving from man to man. No matter how much money I had, I had my mother's traits.

LONELINESS AND DESPAIR

The more women I had, the more despair I felt. It's a bad feeling when they are gone and you're alone in the bedroom. That was Hell. I felt so soulless. So then you just get more girls in, so you don't have to think about that feeling.

SOMEONE TO HOLD ME

Now I needed someone to hold me, because I felt like a piece of shit. All that energy you would get from those different people was *torture*. Sexual orgies, I didn't even know what the f**k was going on in there.

SOMEONE TO MOTHER ME

I had sex with women, hoping it would give me intimacy. I was probably looking for someone to mother me. My whole life I was looking for love from my mother. She never gave love to a man, she gave them headaches, she scolded them. I never saw my mother kiss a man or anyone kiss her forehead. A man for her was just to be used.

POOR AND HAPPY

I'm happy I don't have money, nobody calls, nobody bothers me, nobody is after me, it's so peaceful. *This is rich!*

THE JOY OF THE GOOD

We are still discussing love, but in a positive, happy way.

'Love is the joy of the Good,
the wonder of the Wise
the amazement of the Gods.'

Love like you have never been hurt

Have a wonderful life, darling.

EMOTIONAL, SENSITIVE PEOPLE

Emotional, sensitive people are immature, they can't think. They make decisions 'on the hoof' rather than from the head. Such men are unpredictable, hard to rely on, or even dangerous. They act the way to achieve their ends. They can't be bothered to care about others' feelings.

PAIN IN YOUR HEART

With pain in your heart, there's no room for peace to enter. Welcome pain as a necessary teacher in life. Welcome peace by forgetting and moving on.

HAPPY PEOPLE

Happy people are more loving and forgiving, more open, willing to help.

USE OUR TIME ON EARTH

To use our time on Earth well is to serve others, or at least, to refrain from hurting them. Discover meaning in your life.

DON'T THINK TOO MUCH

Don't think too much, you will be free from anger, guilt, sadness, depression. You're not paid to think, are you? In healthy body, negative emotions have a short life span.

ACCEPT THE UNACCEPTABLE

Some murderers on Death Row waiting for execution experience peace and deep joy in the last moments of their lives. They enter a state of grace, a complete release from the past, thanks to the act of surrender. Deep suffering can lead to deep peace.

LIFE IS RIDICULOUS

Almost everything is life is ridiculous. *Why worry!* Look up and laugh, and love and live!

GOD'S DESIRE FOR US

God's desire for us is to flourish.

OLD AGE

Old age can be beautifully mystical and profound. Let's enjoy it!

THE WORLD WILL KEEP ON TURNING

The world will keep on turning without his father. He has to accept it! His father closed the door on the rest of the world.

SIMPLICITY

In simplicity lies *truth* and *power*. Money is where it all gets real.

INSOMNIA

I was tired but my mind wouldn't let me sleep (intrusive thoughts). If you allow it, it will blow your life apart.

NERVOUSNESS

If people see you're not in control, they will eat you for lunch. It's OK to be nervous, just don't let it show.

TO LOVE BRAVELY

To love bravely is the best. If things get bad to say bravely goodbye is the best too!

END OF RELATIONSHIP

That kind of loneliness you could die from, that bites into your bones.

ON LEAVING PRISON

I felt God was around, the whole world had changed. I wanted to cry, I wanted to laugh. It was almost too much.

A MOTHER'S LOVE

A mother's love is something
That no one can explain
It's made of deep devotion
And of sacrifice and pain

MY LOGICAL MIND

My logical mind is my treasure and my weapon. I must look after it. *No intrusive thoughts for long.* Just peace and silence.

SOMEONE HAS TO START

The famous psychologist Alfred Adler is very encouraging when we can't get support in numbers:

'Someone has to start. Other people might not be cooperative but it's not connected to you. My advice is this: you should start with no regard to whether others are cooperative or not.'

TO KNOW HOW TO GROW OLD

To know how to grow old is the master-work of Wisdom, and one of the most difficult chapters in the great art of living.

LOST LITTLE BOYS

Adler was interested in locating 'lost little boys' hiding behind their beers and violence, not talking about their emotional wounds, their motto:

'Society f****d us, so f**k them.;

READERS AND THINKERS

Readers are plentiful and thinkers are rare.

THE CORE OF STOICISM

Love of wisdom is the core of stoicism. Our wonderful Queen is the greatest role model. Wisdom is her strength!

COURAGE

'We need more courage to live than to die.'

Albert Camus

HUMAN EVIL

Human evil comes from the human heart and darkness of the soul.

STAGE OF FOOLS

'When we are born we cry that we are come to this great stage of fools.'

William Shakespeare, *King Lear*

THINK HAPPY

Remember summer songs and autumn colours. Have faith in the goodness of life. Life is a beautiful, magical thing!

GOOD WILL OF MANY

You can't be trusted if you ill treat your own family. We need the good will of many to make a difference in the world.

SELF-INTEREST IN DOING EVIL

Self-interest in doing evil can give a kind of emotional excitement. Evil people are not mad – they know what they're doing!

KNOWLEDGE, LEARNING AND WISDOM

'May I be aware, in everything I do, that Knowledge comes from Learning and Wisdom comes from you [God].'

H.S. Rice

TAKE THE HORROR OUT OF EVERY PROBLEM

Take the horror out of every problem.
Don't make it too big a tragedy.
Good and bad are part of life.
A problem can be a blessing in disguise.
No law against betrayal.
You will be betrayed again.

ALWAYS EXPRESS TRUE FEELINGS

Repressed feelings will come back to haunt you. Face problems and deal with them, no matter how much it hurts. Pain is for the living, the dead don't feel. It's not about winning, it's about standing up to evil. To survive Hell is the greatest satisfaction of a man!

SOMETIMES IT'S BETTER TO CALL IT QUITS

As Nelson Mandela said, 'It doesn't pay to fight over every issue. Sometimes it's better to call it quits.' It's good to separate important from less important and deal with the important ones only. Be good to yourself, there's more to life than fighting for 'justice'. And something more, to surrender it means going over to the winning side. By this, you too can claim victory.

COMPLEX HUMANITY

Humans are complex creatures and people have a myriad of motives.

LET IT GO

When I get home a bit drunk, why don't you ignore me? Go to the other end of the house and don't stick the needle in, don't press the wrong button. I will be fine in the morning.

PRESSURES

The pressures that had driven her to drink. She just couldn't stop. Human behaviour can be fragile and unpredictable, and often at the mercy of the situation. Not getting what you want is sometimes a wonderful stroke of luck!

PROBLEM OF UPBRINGING

Some men are not interested in women as women; problem of upbringing, a sort of disease!

EVIL

I never knew a beautiful, attractive young woman could have so much evil in her.

GOODNESS

Goodness can be found in the middle of Hell. Never despair, never lose hope. Believe in yourself.

SILENCE

Silence can be power – taking control.
Silence can also be weakness – afraid to tell the truth.

WISDOM AND CHARACTER

Wisdom can be an element of personal character that enables one to distinguish the wise from the unwise. Some are born wise. Wisdom will never let you down. It's your best friend. Don't mix with fools

HAVE FAITH IN HUMAN NATURE

Have faith in human nature, in your own nature, and in the world itself. Learn to live with painful truth, i.e. 'there's no justice in our world' – not to accept it, but to live with it. Calm your heart.

THE LIGHTS OF HOME

'I can see somebody there
Loving eyes and silver hair
I can see her kneel in prayer
Beneath the lights of home.'

TO BE A PARENT

To be a parent is to teach your child to live without you.

A LETTER

It's amazing what a letter can do. Put all your unhappiness in writing, they will have to take you seriously! The letter speaks and communicates with more expressive power.

DISCOVER YOUR WISDOM

We all have our own wisdom. We just have to discover and use it.

SECRETS

If you are doing something in secret, expect to be betrayed. Be realistic, be wise about human nature. Our secrets are as sick as we are.

BENJAMIN FRANKLIN

Franklin published the Wisdom magazine: *Poor Richard's Almanac*. Here are three quotations from it:

- → Beware of little expenses.
- → A small leak will sink a big ship
- → A penny saved is a penny earned.

A LIE HAS TO BE SELF-SUFFICIENT

'A lie has to be self-sufficient. It can not appeal to anything else for support. Lies must stand on their own, as a work of art. A fine lie has to be its own evidence. If a man can't produce an evidence in support of his lie. He might as well speak the truth at once.'

Oscar Wilde

FOLLY

Folly is sweet, if well-timed. Mingle a little folly with your Wisdom – a little nonsense now and then... is characterised by the best of men.

WRITING BOOKS WELL

Of writing books well, be sure the secret lies in Wisdom; therefore study to be wise. A bird doesn't sing because he has an answer: it sings because it has a song.

LETTING GO OF MONEY

To let go of my money produced the most rewarding stage of my life. My spirit is strong, sweet and loving. Money is at the bottom of my list.

NO ONE CAN HEAR OUR THOUGHTS

No one can hear our thoughts. Otherwise no one would talk to anyone. Not everybody's heart is capable of loving. It's a global issue.

BEAUTIFUL YOUTH

Isn't all youth beautiful?

PUNCTUALITY

Punctuality is the politeness of kings.

ABRAHAM LINCOLN

I would like to introduce you to a great man and to encourage you to think of him as a great role model for all young people. Abraham Lincoln grew up in great poverty – a log cabin with three walls only. He lost his mother when he was nine and missed her very much because his father wasn't very nice to him. He taught himself to read and write and to be a lawyer. Instead of going out drinking with his friends, he was always reading and asking people for books. The Bible and *Aesop's Fables* were his favourites. Little Abe was 16th President of the USA – remembered for his honesty, compassion, and character. He was very humble – a wonderful human being.

POLITICIANS

What would you think about a politician who became a rebel in his own party? Should he go and join the opposition, his ex-enemy? A good politician is/should be bigger than his office. Politicians are only for a season. What are they trying to achieve? They often betray the people who elected them.

DOMESTIC INSTABILITY IN CHILDHOOD

We create it for our children. A home should be a place of safety and love – not a place of anxiety, stress, sadness, pain. Our children need to know and understand what's going on. They need to be told, in plain language, what's happening. It will give them self-confidence, self-worth, they won't feel responsible for the family problems – they will avoid mental health problems as adults.

SURVIVING PRISON

Have you ever wondered how a human being can survive years in prison? Some commit suicide; others have the capacity to anaesthetise themselves. Horrible becomes normal. They lose a sense of horror. It no longer bothers them, they get used to it. There is a natural tendency in human organisations to become more primitive as a way of survival. One of humanity's greatest attributes is its capacity for suffering. Prison is worse than murder. Avoid it at any price. Can you imagine Nelson Mandela spending 27 years in prison? I can't!

ACCEPTING ROUTINE

Let's talk again about life and accepting our routine chores – which will often cause depression for some of us. 'What's the point?' some of us might think. Work, home – the same every day, not much excitement. Life is a gift, and it's ouir responsibility to create our own excitement. We're talking about our attitudes, insecurities, the Wisdom of our emotions and thinking. Should the sun get depressed rising and setting every day? Should birds be depressed looking for worms and seeds every day and stop foraging for them? Stay cheerful! Our world isn't a paradise, but it's still good to be alive!

DIGNIFIED POVERTY

The common argument that crime is caused by poverty is a kind of slander on the poor! People can be very greedy: the more they have the more they want and will do anything for money. I'm poor because I'm honest, a wise old man will tell you.

IN THE DARK

Keeping a man in the dark, not knowing what will happen to him next, will destroy man's Mind and Soul. A man needs something to focus on. A man needs hope. His mind will help him to stay alive, to find the reason for living.

BE HUMBLE

Be humble. How do you know that your knowledge is final?

THE GREATEST CRIME

The sin that humans commit are not their greatest crime. Temptations are powerful and people are weak! The greatest crime is that people can turn at every moment and *do not do so*!

TO HAVE A DREAM

You need to have a dream to get up in the morning.

MONEY AND TRUE WEALTH

Some have money. Others are rich in mind and heart.

POWER, WISDOM AND COMPASSION

Some power has to bow to Wisdom and Compassion

WHEN GODS WANT TO DESTROY

When gods want to destroy the powerful and evil, they take their brains away.

DEALING WITH PEOPLE

Try to behave with a mild affection towards people so that they won't think they own you. Don't expect too much of them and don't offer too much either. You will keep yourself out of trouble and remain fully human. Do only what your duty is, that's good enough.

SOCIABLE WISDOM

'I'm born for company and friendship' Montaigne wrote. He loved to mingle. Conversation is something he enjoyed more than any other pleasure. Nothing of a serious nature, just joking with friends with a kind, friendly spirit. Social grace of this kind, Montaigne thought, should be encouraged in children from an early age to bring them out of their private worlds. Montaigne loved open debates, a way of getting to know people. He liked being contradicted – it helped him in his thinking.

WEAKNESS

Almost all cruelty springs from weakness. A strong, confident people wouldn't think of hurting others. They are happy in their own skin and will walk away from a fight. If someone plays dirty with you, should you play dirty with them? Would you like to get dirty too? Value yourself, you know to know better!

WHAT DO YOU MEAN?

Ask the question: what do you mean? to avoid misunderstanding. Wisdom offers physical and emotional health. Show understanding of the problem first; put your points across later. You will be trusted.

SPIRITUALITY

The quality of human spirit – love, compassion, patience, tolerance, forgiveness, sense of responsibility, harmony, humility – brings happiness to self and others.

CHILD ABUSE

Child abuse is the assault upon a sensitive individual by an ugly society! 'Some are born to sweet delight, some are born to endless night' (William Blake). The horror of life, terror of existence, senseless everyday stupidity, pain of childhood can be lodged in your mind and in your body. It can be activated by events in the present. Pain can feed on pain and it hurts more. A recent death of a friend will remind you about the death of your brother in the past.

DON'T OVERUSE YOUR IMAGE

If you want to be hugely successful you have to stay hugely humble. The more humble you are the more personal power you have. Your photo in a magazine is no big deal – relax.

HONESTY AND HEALTH

The healthiest people are the most honest in their behaviour. Their pattern of thinking is the least distorted. Psychopathy is overwhelming and can be scary. Truth likes open dealings.

A SENSITIVE PERSON

He was quite a sensitive person who felt deeply about the passing of the seasons, children growing up and leaving, the transcience of existence, vulnerability of pain, tenderness.

OCD

Obsessive compulsive disorder. Because of his childhood experience he became a very neat, methodical adult.

PSYCHIATRY

Nothing is *bad* – no thoughts, no wishes, no feelings. Only what we actually do is bad. We need to face things that are painful, very painful, and not run away. We need to talk to people we trust. There's no other way.

SYMPTOMS OF REPRESSED FEELINGS

Anger, hurt, sadness, guilt, addiction. Do something about it. Talk, share.

PEOPLE OF LIE

Evil people always hide their motives with lies, repeatedly, routinely. They are 'people of Lie'. Even bringing their children to see a psychiatrist was a Lie. They wanted to look good, nothing else. They didn't really care about their children.

DENIAL

Some people deny humiliating self-knowledge. Nazis denied till the very end, killing millions and keeping their perfect moral self-images, denying their own faults.

OLD PEOPLE

An old person can be peaceful, accepting of themself and others, because they have learned about their own faults. Otherwise they will forever remain an angry old person!

LOVING AND LEARNING WISDOM

You need to love it and learn it. You don't become wise by chance.

THE UNKNOWN

We are all frightened of the unknown. Today make the most of small opportunities and tasks – they could just be the start of great things.

WHAT CAN ENDANGER THE WORLD?

Our carelessness, hostilities. pride, wilful ignorance – are all that endanger our world. Wisdom will give us sanity and confidence. We need a kinder, more caring society.

REJECTION

To reject someone – do it nicely, without vengeance. Somebody is asking you for a favour and your answer is no. Being rejected, I would tell the person: 'Be kind, you don't reject me. You reject my request. I do understand you! But please, at least give me an alternative, not just unkind silence.'

HUMAN EVIL

Human evil is dangerous. It can also destroy a healthy person who remains too long in its presence. Children, victims of human evil in their family home or other environment can grow up to become psychologically damaged adults. Human evil is a form of mental illness, it's about lies, deceit, betrayal, etc. Unfortunately evil wears a mask of sanity. Evil people think of themselves as being superior. Mental pain can not be adjusted and madness is the last stage of human degradation.

REINCARNATION OF EVIL

The Asmat people living in Indonesia apparently believe that evil people come back reincarnated as crocodiles. Who knew!

AM I GOOD ENOUGH?

Do you ever worry 'Am I good enough?' Let's say, for a girl, do you ever worry: am I pretty enough? The answer is: you don't have to be pretty, no! no! no! Babies and young children are pretty by just being babies – no teeth, no hair. Youth is beauty in itself. Lovely character, warm personality, that's all that matters. A kind man is a handsome man and will treat his woman well. It takes a special man to stay with the same woman for long. Why? Because a good musician doesn't need two violins to play good music!

TO BE GOOD ENOUGH

To be good enough is easy, if that's what we want! We need to control our impulses, our demons. We don't benefit from hurting others and that is wrong. It's our choice who we want to be – to be good enough or 'bad'. In an ideal world, our parents would be our role models. With their help and love every day, we could make the best of who we are and what we are!

OTHER 'GOOD ENOUGH'S

+ Do your parents make you feel good enough?
+ Do you feel good enough at school?
+ Do you feel good enough living in your adopted country?
+ Do you feel good enough in your marriage?
+ Do you feel good enough at intimacy?
+ Do you feel good enough at growing old?

NOTHING BELONGS TO US

Nothing belongs to us completely, finally. A job is ended, children leave home. We learn to make peace with our destiny. We might feel sad, but also serene. Nothing disturbs us. We value life for what it has given us, not for any promise of tomorrow. *We conquer time by accepting it.*

LIFE IS A GIFT

I would like for humans to realise that we are here for a short time only. We could live in peace and harmony. No point in fighting or being unkind.

Life is a gift and it's a beautiful word.

TO CHALLENGE

To challenge is a solution to all our problems – including greed, anger, stupidity!

WE ARE BIGGER THAN OUR PROBLEMS

Human beings are creative – animals are not. We can alter (in most cases) the course of our lives. We mustn't lose our moral compass. *We are bigger than our problems and our thoughts.*

ADOPTED CHILDREN

It can be very difficult for them. They might feel that something is missing, like reading a book without the first four pages. You never stop thinking about what might have been. Adopted children fear unbelonging because their adoptive parents are not 'real' – they might just disappear. They often feel that they are alone. If you have a friend who was adopted, try to understand, try to tell them: 'You're special, you were chosen by your adoptive parents. Your birth mother feels sad today, thinking 'My baby boy is eleven today. I do hope he's happy.'

POST-TRAUMATIC STRESS DISORDER

He suffered shocking emotional trauma and Post-Traumatic Stress Disorder. It shouldn't be called 'disorder' because it's a normal reaction to feel this way. He was brutal to his family, hated everything, experienced a mysterious skin disease, felt 'safe' with alcohol. The healing process can take a long time.

MARRIAGE IS HARD WORK

Marriage is hard work. Two people need to be committed. 'May you be married as long as it's good' not 'till death us do part'. People change, have emotional problems. The person you married at the age of twenty is not the same person now, very often. When your marriage can't be saved, try to make your divorce as friendly as possible for your children's sake.

CALLING A TAIL A LEG

'How many legs does a dog have, if you call the tail a leg?'

Four! Calling a tail a leg doesn't make it a leg.

Abraham Lincoln

LISTEN

Listen carefully to what people say. Don't be anybody's fool. And what about TV commercials? Have modest doubt.

A STATE OF BEING

Love is state of being. It's deep inside you, not outside. You can never lose it and it can never leave you. You just need your partner to share their love with you. Don't cry for too long if your partner leaves. A good person is waiting for you round the corner. Don't despair.

WORDS

Words are the most powerful and dangerous drug used by mankind. You might know the saying, 'Sticks and stones...' Yes, words can hurt you in a very bad way.

APPEAL

People in high places, well educated, etc. can make mistakes in their judgement. For that reason we have the gift to make an appeal. It's our right to question any decision that involves our life. Don't think twice, just do it, when you need it!

WISE THOUGHTS

All starts with thinking, followed by feeling and action. Start having wise thoughts and you will feel happy. The choice is ours, no one to blame.

WHEN YOU MEET A FRIEND

When you meet a friend, don't start with 'Do you know what?' and tell them sad news. Try something happy, cheerful. It could life their spirits – something we all need desperately today.

THOSE WHO HAVE PARTED THIS WORLD

Those who have parted this world don't disappear. They walk beside us each and every day. I refuse to think that my father is dead. I talk to him very often. I ask him for his advice in important matters. It's very comforting. And I do believe that one day we will meet again. It's my choice to believe.

A LETTER TO A LAW FIRM

Today I am writing to tell you that I feel happy to forgive you all your brutality. I was a fool to trust you. You don't ask for my forgiveness. I do it for myself. Hating you is very painful and does nothing good for my health. Five years of Hell from you is more than enough. Enjoy the money that's not yours. Spend it well!

WONDER IN EVERYTHING

There's wonder in everything in life: painful tears have their beauty too. We love our mother; she loves us. Grieving is beautiful; grieving is love. We are lucky to experience the pain. Some of us didn't know their mothers. Tears wash our pain away – we need to cry a lot. We need to have compassion for ourselves. We're little orphans here on Earth, now. I want to believe that one day we will see our mothers again. For now, you're a little child crying for your mother.

THE WISDOM OF SHAKESPEARE

Since all is well, keep it so; wake not a sleeping wolf

*

A peace above all earthly dignities,
A still and quiet mind

*

Kindness, nobler ever than revenge

*

Poor and content is rich, and rich enough

*

Life is a tale told by an idiot
Full of sound and fury, signifying nothing

*

Oh gentlemen, the time of life is short

*

Truth is truth, to the end of reckoning

*

Oh, what may man within hide
Though angel on the outward side

*

We can profit, by losing our prayers

*

Death – the undiscovered country

*

The dead are well
The old bees die, the young possess their hive

*

To weep is to make less the depth of grief

*

There's nothing either good or bad, but thinking makes it so

*

What fools these mortals be!

*

Sigh no more ladies, sigh no more
Men were deceivers ever
One foot in sea, and one on shore,
To one thing constant never

*

Simplicity and its beauty
To throw a perfume on the violet
Is wasteful and ridiculous excess

*

My crown is in my heart, not on my head
Not decked with diamonds and Indian stones

Not to be seen, my crown is called content
A crown it is that seldom kings enjoy

*

Though it be honest
It is never good to bring bad news

SUMMARY

TO INTRODUCE YOUNG PEOPLE TO NEW THINKING AND FEELING

- ◆ Emotional intelligence (EI) and Wisdom can determine life success more than IQ
- ◆ A wise man knows the meaning of his words
- ◆ We live in an imperfect world
- ◆ One wisdom can save us
- ◆ Fame: game of mugs, empty bubble
- ◆ You can't be benefit from hurting others – be kind
- ◆ Money can't buy you happiness
- ◆ You know better, you do better
- ◆ Remember to think and to reason
- ◆ Have modest doubt about everything and everybody
- ◆ Be emotionally self-aware and authentic
- ◆ Speak openly about your feelings
- ◆ Try to understand others and forgive

- But remember: Wisdom never lies
- Truth is simple but often painful
- Never lose hope
- You're just as good as others, if not better
- We are all very special
- If you can't change it, accept it – anything else would be madness
- There's a limit to spending: we don't need more things we need Wisdom
- Sex is not love – it's sex
- Never act on confused emotions such as anger – you might regret it
- Be happy in your own quiet way
- Pain can be far too deep for tears
- Reckless courage is not a good idea
- Love all, trust few, harm no one
- Don't mix with fools
- Live well, laugh often, love much
- Exercise self-discipline
- Take the horror out of every problem
- Things are not as bad as they might look
- No law against betrayal – you will be betrayed again, take care
- Good and bad are a part of life
- God is in Heaven, all is well with the world

EPILOGUE

CHILDREN'S PRAYER

Dear Lord,

I would like to pray for all the people that I love but who live far away. Tonight with them my thoughts I share. Please keep them in your loving care, each night and every day.

THE SADNESS OF MODERN LIFE

The sadness of modern life is missing our families.

FACING CONFLICT

Facing overwhelming conflict produced greatness and beauty.

GOD IS YOUR VINDICATOR

God is your Vindicator, your Defender. He will settle your case and repay everything the enemy has stolen from you.

You have to release those who have wronged you, from what you thing they owe you. That is true forgiveness – freeing others, so that you can be free.

PEACE IN YOUR MIND AND HEART

Enjoy a simple happy life, with precious peace in your Mind and in your Heart. Love all, trust few, hurt no one. Be in control of your thoughts and emotions. *Be Wise!*

APPENDIX I

To the Right Honourable Boris Johnson, PM

Dear Mr Johnson

Re: How to deal with racism: friendly advice

1. Racism is nothing more than ignorance. It's hard for us to accept people who are different from us in any way.

2. People are good or bad. It had nothing to do with their skin colour or race.

3. Let's raise our new generation, guiding young people with love and logic.

4. We need to trust human nature when hoping for changes for a better world.

5. Human nature is very complex. We are all a bit

mad. Some of us realise it. No one is perfect. We're only human and come from different backgrounds.

6. We all have one thing in common: we all want to be happy and not suffer.

7. At my school we were taught how to learn, how to think and reason, how to love, how to care. School is about more than just ABC. Teachers affect eternity. They shape young minds.

8. Benjamin Franklin said:

> `We need knowledge that will profit Society, will improve moral and economic status. The knowledge that is both useful and social, knowledge about honour, dignity, happiness. School plays a big part in it. We need enthusiastic teachers.

9. Erasmus, the great Renaissance thinker, said:

> 'The best hope of a nation lies in the proper education of its youth.'

10. Racism is human evil. It comes from our hearts and the darkness of our souls. We are all capable of evil.

11. We don't have to love everyone and not everybody has to love us. Some of us are quietly racist and don't let others know about it. But to accept other people, irrespective of their race or colour is called tolerance.

12. We're all the same. We were all born the same way and we will all die the same way.

13. Sometimes we have to accept being different. Everything else would be madness. It could affect our mental health very badly.

14. Bullies are bullies because they enjoy upsetting us. We mustn't give them the satisfaction.

15. Human evil is as old as time. Have you heard about Aesop. Wonderful man who lived 2,500 years ago.

16. Aesop's Fables, revised version by Susie Moore (2017), page 138, 'The North Wind and the Sun' jas great Wisdom:

'Persuasion is better than force.'

17. We need to raise our capacity for love and understanding, instead of punishing people for being racists and bad!

18. People are good at heart – they're just misguided!

19. Tell your teenage child:

'Please be back home by 10 pm, it's for your own safety'

is better than:

'Be home by 10 pm, otherwise you'll be grounded.'

20. We all can make a difference in our unkind world. It's everybody's moral duty.

21. My late husband was Hindu, a very good looking very kind man. His parents were very cruel. They favoured his sisters whose skin was whiter.

22. Would you call this 'racism in the family'? His whiter sisters would go out with his parents, while he stayed at home. How cruel and sad that was!

I am sending a copy of this letter to the Rt. Hon. Teresa May, our ex-Prime Minister. Women tend to be better at understanding human emotions and I like her very much. I'm also sending a copy to the Labour Leader, the Rt. Hon. Sir Keir Starmer, to the Duke and Duchess of C Cambridge, who do care, and to The Times and Sunday Times.

Whether I'm right or wrong I don't know but it feels good in my old, battered heart (I'm aged 79).

We can all make a difference – we just need to be willing!

Warmest regards and thank you for reading my writing.

Yania Braun
November 2021
Oxford

PS: Indifference to other person's suffering. Racism is a human evil. Human evil is mental disorder. Mentally healthy people do care: they have a conscience. Racists are mentally disturbed.

APPENDIX II

CAN YOU COME BACK FROM THE GRAVE?

On 13 May 2014, at the age of 71½ and after five years of volunteering with young people in New Zealand, I was unlawfully arrested and snatched from my new Kiwi husband Graeme, who needed me. My visa was valid for another five months; my case officer was a Russian lady named Olesya.

Deportation was one thing but violation of basic human rights was another. The British High Commission in Wellington performed a human miracle in caring and after 90 days on remand I was on a plane back to England.

In the Auckland prison for women I was suicidal: the fear of going mad was killing me. The 'at risk' place was worse than murder; I was not allowed to wear knickers or shoes; there was a bare, stone floor; my reading glasses were taken away from me; I was forced to eat with my fingers. Seven days of this and I died seven times!

I wrote begging, plaintive letters to important

officials while in prison. John Key was the Prime Minister. His Secretary replied, 'The PM trusts his Ministers and won't intervene.'

To fast forward the story: on 12 December 2016 John Key resigned. Before this he had sacked two Ministers for Immigration and the New Zealand High Commissioner to London. I wrote emails and letters to many important people. It was so unnecessary but with God's help I did 'come back from the grave', and since then I have done my very best to help others. My emotional loyalty to wonderful England dominates my life.

Our beautiful Queen – it brings tears to my eyes every time I think about her great kindness and caring and I pray for her health every day!

Prisoner No. 807 18383

INDEX

We don't receive Wisdom,

we must discover it for ourselves,

after journey through the wilderness,

a struggle and a victory,

which no one else can make for us,

which no one can spare us,

for our Wisdom is the point of view,

from which we come at last

to regard the World".

Marcel Proust.

" Injustice of our World,

it can be very, very scary,

being innocent, sometimes

can mean very little or nothing...

Choose your friends well,

listen to them, but trust

the Wisdom in your Heart

to keep you Safe and Strong,

be always Wise, think for yourself,

don't follow, you're not a "Sheep".
Sheep ".

Prisoner's No: 807 183 83
New Zealand 2014.

Printed in Great Britain
by Amazon

37357136R00106